The Illuminated Omer Counting Book

The Illuminated Omer Counting Book

A beautiful and practical way to count the Omer

James N. Gershfield

The Illuminated Omer Counting Book

Written and illustrated by James N. Gershfield

Published by  Scribal Scion Publishing

First Edition, published in 2023

ISBN-13: 979-8-88665-000-6 (paperback)

Scribal Scion Publishing is an imprint of
Scribal Scion Publishing LLC, Teaneck NJ, USA

This book is lovingly dedicated to the memory of my late father, Rabbi Edward M. Gershfield - teacher, preacher and scribe.

Please visit our website to learn more about us, our mission and our books: **https://scribalscionpublishing.com**

Introduction

This book makes it easy and enjoyable to count the Omer. It is designed to be displayed in your home or office. Just turn the page each day to see the current day and week of the Omer in English and Hebrew, along with an artistic rendering of the count in Hebrew letters.

For many centuries, Jewish scribes created beautiful illuminated manuscripts of various religious texts in order to enhance the reader's enjoyment. It is with the same purpose in mind that I created this practical and artistic, Illuminated Omer Counting Book, in order to enhance the performance of the Mitzvah (religious obligation) to count the Omer between the Jewish holidays of Pesach and Shavuot. However, instead of using a feather pen, ink and paper, as a traditional scribe would have done, I used a computer mouse and software to create the Hebrew letters and the artwork.

May this book help motivate you to observe the counting of the Omer every day during the 49 days of the counting, and may it help you to fulfill the Mitzvah in a spirit of joy and happiness.

How to Use This Book

In order to get the most out of this book, it is best to use some kind of book stand to display the book with the pages open to the current day of the Omer. If you don't have a book stand, you can simply put a bookmark into the book at the page corresponding to the current day of the Omer and move the bookmark each day to the next pair of pages.

This book does not contain the blessing that is normally recited before counting the Omer each night. Please refer to a Siddur (Jewish Prayer Book) or search online for the text of the blessing.

What This Book is Not

This book is not intended to teach you the laws of counting the Omer, nor is it intended to tell you which blessings to say or how to say them. Also, this book is not intended to explain the deeper meaning of the counting of the Omer, or which verse in the Torah the Mitzvah of counting the Omer is based on.

It simply provides a beautiful and practical way to keep track of the current day during the counting of the Omer.

Day 1

**Today is One Day
of the Omer**

הַיוֹם יוֹם אֶחָד לָעֹמֶר

Day 2

Today is Two Days of the Omer

הַיוֹם שְׁנֵי יָמִים לָעֹמֶר

Day 3

**Today is Three Days
of the Omer**

הַיּוֹם שְׁלֹשָׁה יָמִים לָעֹמֶר

Day 4

**Today is Four Days
of the Omer**

הַיוֹם אַרְבָּעָה יָמִים לָעֹמֶר

Day 5

**Today is Five Days
of the Omer**

הַיּוֹם חֲמִשָּׁה יָמִים לָעֹמֶר

Day 6

**Today is Six Days
of the Omer**

הַיּוֹם שִׁשָּׁה יָמִים לָעֹמֶר

Day 7

1 Week

Today is Seven Days, which are One Week, of the Omer

הַיּוֹם שִׁבְעָה יָמִים שֶׁהֵם שָׁבוּעַ אֶחָד לָעֹמֶר

Day 8

1 Week, 1 Day

**Today is Eight Days,
which are One Week
and One Day,
of the Omer**

הַיּוֹם שְׁמוֹנָה יָמִים שֶׁהֵם
שָׁבוּעַ אֶחָד וְיוֹם אֶחָד לָעֹמֶר

Day 9

1 Week, 2 Days

Today is Nine Days,
which are One Week
and Two Days,
of the Omer

הַיוֹם תִּשְׁעָה יָמִים שֶׁהֵם
שָׁבוּעַ אֶחָד וּשְׁנֵי יָמִים לָעֹמֶר

Day 10

1 Week, 3 Days

Today is Ten Days,
which are One Week
and Three Days,
of the Omer

הַיוֹם עֲשָׂרָה יָמִים שֶׁהֵם
שָׁבוּעַ אֶחָד וּשְׁלשָׁה יָמִים לָעֹמֶר

Day 11

1 Week, 4 Days

**Today is Eleven Days,
which are One Week
and Four Days,
of the Omer**

הַיּוֹם אַחַד עָשָׂר יוֹם שֶׁהֵם
שָׁבוּעַ אֶחָד וְאַרְבָּעָה יָמִים לָעֹמֶר

Day 12

1 Week, 5 Days

Today is Twelve Days,
which are One Week
and Five Days,
of the Omer

הַיוֹם שְׁנֵים עָשָׂר יוֹם שֶׁהֵם
שָׁבוּעַ אֶחָד וַחֲמִשָּׁה יָמִים לָעֹמֶר

Day 13

1 Week, 6 Days

**Today is Thirteen Days,
which are One Week
and Six Days,
of the Omer**

הַיוֹם שְׁלשָׁה עָשָׂר יוֹם שֶׁהֵם
שָׁבוּעַ אֶחָד וְשִׁשָׁה יָמִים לָעֹמֶר

Day 14

2 Weeks

**Today is Fourteen Days,
which are Two Weeks,
of the Omer**

הַיוֹם אַרְבָּעָה עָשָׂר יוֹם שֶׁהֵם
שְׁנֵי שָׁבוּעוֹת לָעֹמֶר

Day 15

2 Weeks, 1 Day

**Today is Fifteen Days,
which are Two Weeks
and One Day,
of the Omer**

הַיוֹם חֲמִשָּׁה עָשָׂר יוֹם שֶׁהֵם
שְׁנֵי שָׁבוּעוֹת וְיוֹם אֶחָד לָעֹמֶר

Day 16

2 Weeks, 2 Days

Today is Sixteen Days,
which are Two Weeks
and Two Days,
of the Omer

הַיוֹם שִׁשָּׁה עָשָׂר יוֹם שֶׁהֵם
שְׁנֵי שָׁבוּעוֹת וּשְׁנֵי יָמִים לָעֹמֶר

Day 17

2 Weeks, 3 Days

Today is Seventeen Days,
which are Two Weeks
and Three Days,
of the Omer

הַיּוֹם שִׁבְעָה עָשָׂר יוֹם שֶׁהֵם
שְׁנֵי שָׁבוּעוֹת וּשְׁלֹשָׁה יָמִים לָעֹמֶר

Day 18

2 Weeks, 4 Days

**Today is Eighteen Days,
which are Two Weeks
and Four Days,
of the Omer**

הַיוֹם שְׁמוֹנָה עָשָׂר יוֹם שֶׁהֵם
שְׁנֵי שָׁבוּעוֹת וְאַרְבָּעָה יָמִים לָעֹמֶר

Day 19

2 Weeks, 5 Days

**Today is Nineteen Days,
which are Two Weeks
and Five Days,
of the Omer**

הַיוֹם תִּשְׁעָה עָשָׂר יוֹם שֶׁהֵם
שְׁנֵי שָׁבוּעוֹת וַחֲמִשָּׁה יָמִים לָעֹמֶר

Day 20

2 Weeks, 6 Days

**Today is Twenty Days,
which are Two Weeks
and Six Days,
of the Omer**

הַיוֹם עֶשְׂרִים יוֹם שֶׁהֵם
שְׁנֵי שָׁבוּעוֹת וְשִׁשָּׁה יָמִים לָעֹמֶר

Day 21

3 Weeks

Today is Twenty One Days,
which are Three Weeks,
of the Omer

הַיוֹם אֶחָד וְעֶשְׂרִים יוֹם שֶׁהֵם
שְׁלֹשָׁה שָׁבוּעוֹת לָעֹמֶר

Day 22

3 Weeks, 1 Day

Today is Twenty Two Days,
which are Three Weeks
and One Day,
of the Omer

הַיּוֹם שְׁנַיִם וְעֶשְׂרִים יוֹם שֶׁהֵם
שְׁלֹשָׁה שָׁבוּעוֹת וְיוֹם אֶחָד לָעֹמֶר

Day 23

3 Weeks, 2 Days

Today is Twenty Three Days,
which are Three Weeks
and Two Days,
of the Omer

הַיוֹם שְׁלשָׁה וְעֶשְׂרִים יוֹם שֶׁהֵם
שְׁלשָׁה שָׁבוּעוֹת וּשְׁנֵי יָמִים לָעֹמֶר

Day 24

3 Weeks, 3 Days

Today is Twenty Four Days,
which are Three Weeks
and Three Days,
of the Omer

הַיּוֹם אַרְבָּעָה וְעֶשְׂרִים יוֹם שֶׁהֵם
שְׁלֹשָׁה שָׁבוּעוֹת וּשְׁלֹשָׁה יָמִים לָעֹמֶר

Day 25

3 Weeks, 4 Days

**Today is Twenty Five Days,
which are Three Weeks
and Four Days,
of the Omer**

הַיוֹם חֲמִשָּׁה וְעֶשְׂרִים יוֹם שֶׁהֵם
שְׁלֹשָׁה שָׁבוּעוֹת וְאַרְבָּעָה יָמִים לָעֹמֶר

Day 26

3 Weeks, 5 Days

Today is Twenty Six Days,
which are Three Weeks
and Five Days,
of the Omer

הַיּוֹם שִׁשָּׁה וְעֶשְׂרִים יוֹם שֶׁהֵם
שְׁלֹשָׁה שָׁבוּעוֹת וַחֲמִשָּׁה יָמִים לָעֹמֶר

Day 27

3 Weeks, 6 Days

Today is Twenty Seven Days,
which are Three Weeks
and Six Days,
of the Omer

הַיוֹם שִׁבְעָה וְעֶשְׂרִים יוֹם שֶׁהֵם
שְׁלֹשָׁה שָׁבוּעוֹת וְשִׁשָּׁה יָמִים לָעֹמֶר

Day 28

4 Weeks

**Today is Twenty Eight Days,
which are Four Weeks,
of the Omer**

הַיוֹם שְׁמוֹנָה וְעֶשְׂרִים יוֹם שֶׁהֵם
אַרְבָּעָה שָׁבוּעוֹת לָעֹמֶר

Day 29

4 Weeks, 1 Day

**Today is Twenty Nine Days,
which are Four Weeks
and One Day,
of the Omer**

הַיוֹם תִּשְׁעָה וְעֶשְׂרִים יוֹם שֶׁהֵם
אַרְבָּעָה שָׁבוּעוֹת וְיוֹם אֶחָד לָעֹמֶר

Day 30

4 Weeks, 2 Days

Today is Thirty Days,
which are Four Weeks
and Two Days,
of the Omer

הַיּוֹם שְׁלֹשִׁים יוֹם שֶׁהֵם
אַרְבָּעָה שָׁבוּעוֹת וּשְׁנֵי יָמִים לָעֹמֶר

Day 31

4 Weeks, 3 Days

Today is Thirty One Days,
which are Four Weeks
and Three Days,
of the Omer

הַיוֹם אֶחָד וּשְׁלשִׁים יוֹם שֶׁהֵם
אַרְבָּעָה שָׁבוּעוֹת וּשְׁלשָׁה יָמִים לָעֹמֶר

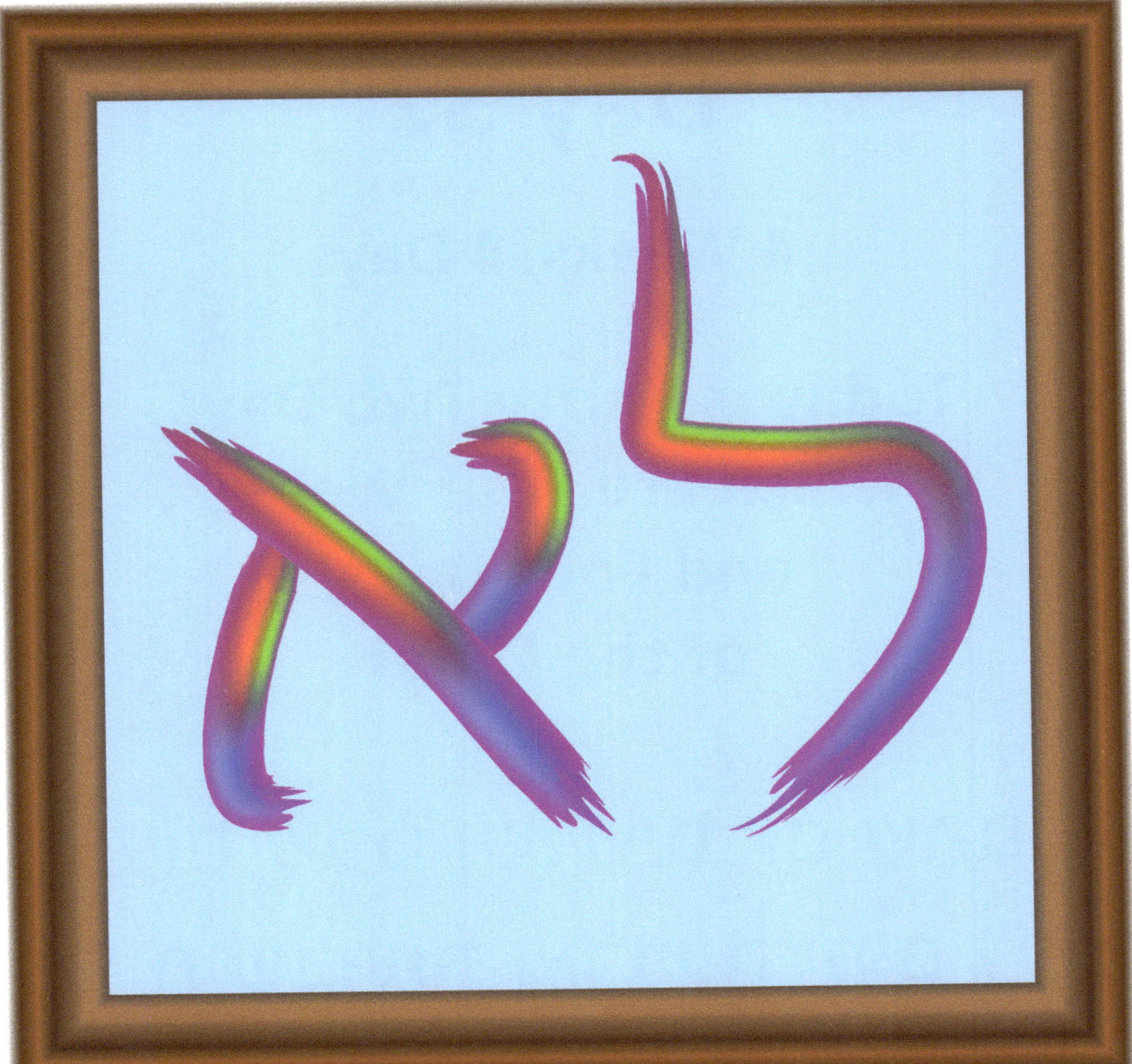

Day 32

4 Weeks, 4 Days

**Today is Thirty Two Days,
which are Four Weeks
and Four Days,
of the Omer**

הַיום שְׁנַיִם וּשְׁלשִׁים יום שֶׁהֵם
אַרְבָּעָה שָׁבוּעוֹת וְאַרְבָּעָה יָמִים לָעֹמֶר

Day 33

4 Weeks, 5 Days

Today is Thirty Three Days,
which are Four Weeks
and Five Days,
of the Omer

הַיוֹם שְׁלֹשָׁה וּשְׁלֹשִׁים יוֹם שֶׁהֵם
אַרְבָּעָה שָׁבוּעוֹת וַחֲמִשָּׁה יָמִים לָעֹמֶר

Lag Ba'Omer

Day 34

4 Weeks, 6 Days

Today is Thirty Four Days,
which are Four Weeks
and Six Days,
of the Omer

הַיוֹם אַרְבָּעָה וּשְׁלשִׁים יוֹם שֶׁהֵם
אַרְבָּעָה שָׁבוּעוֹת וְשִׁשָּׁה יָמִים לָעֹמֶר

Day 35

5 Weeks

**Today is Thirty Five Days,
which are Five Weeks,
of the Omer**

הַיוֹם חֲמִשָּׁה וּשְׁלֹשִׁים יוֹם שֶׁהֵם
חֲמִשָּׁה שָׁבוּעוֹת לָעֹמֶר

Day 36

5 Weeks, 1 Day

**Today is Thirty Six Days,
which are Five Weeks
and One Day,
of the Omer**

הַיוֹם שִׁשָּׁה וּשְׁלשִׁים יוֹם שֶׁהֵם
חֲמִשָּׁה שָׁבוּעוֹת וְיוֹם אֶחָד לָעֹמֶר

Day 37

5 Weeks, 2 Days

Today is Thirty Seven Days,
which are Five Weeks
and Two Days,
of the Omer

הַיּוֹם שִׁבְעָה וּשְׁלֹשִׁים יוֹם שֶׁהֵם
חֲמִשָּׁה שָׁבוּעוֹת וּשְׁנֵי יָמִים לָעֹמֶר

Day 38

5 Weeks, 3 Days

**Today is Thirty Eight Days,
which are Five Weeks
and Three Days,
of the Omer**

הַיּוֹם שְׁמוֹנָה וּשְׁלֹשִׁים יוֹם שֶׁהֵם
חֲמִשָּׁה שָׁבוּעוֹת וּשְׁלֹשָׁה יָמִים לָעֹמֶר

Day 39

5 Weeks, 4 Days

**Today is Thirty Nine Days,
which are Five Weeks
and Four Days,
of the Omer**

הַיוֹם תִּשְׁעָה וּשְׁלֹשִׁים יוֹם שֶׁהֵם
חֲמִשָׁה שָׁבוּעוֹת וְאַרְבָּעָה יָמִים לָעֹמֶר

Day 40

5 Weeks, 5 Days

**Today is Forty Days,
which are Five Weeks
and Five Days,
of the Omer**

הַיּוֹם אַרְבָּעִים יוֹם שֶׁהֵם
חֲמִשָּׁה שָׁבוּעוֹת וַחֲמִשָּׁה יָמִים לָעֹמֶר

Day 41

5 Weeks, 6 Days

Today is Forty One Days,
which are Five Weeks
and Six Days,
of the Omer

הַיּוֹם אֶחָד וְאַרְבָּעִים יוֹם שֶׁהֵם
חֲמִשָּׁה שָׁבוּעוֹת וְשִׁשָּׁה יָמִים לָעֹמֶר

Day 42

6 Weeks

**Today is Forty Two Days,
which are Six Weeks,
of the Omer**

הַיוֹם שְׁנַיִם וְאַרְבָּעִים יוֹם שֶׁהֵם
שִׁשָּׁה שָׁבוּעוֹת לָעֹמֶר

Day 43

6 Weeks, 1 Day

Today is Forty Three Days,
which are Six Weeks
and One Day,
of the Omer

הַיּוֹם שְׁלֹשָׁה וְאַרְבָּעִים יוֹם שֶׁהֵם
שִׁשָּׁה שָׁבוּעוֹת וְיוֹם אֶחָד לָעֹמֶר

Day 44

6 Weeks, 2 Days

Today is Forty Four Days,
which are Six Weeks
and Two Days,
of the Omer

הַיוֹם אַרְבָּעָה וְאַרְבָּעִים יוֹם שֶׁהֵם
שִׁשָּׁה שָׁבוּעוֹת וּשְׁנֵי יָמִים לָעֹמֶר

Day 45

6 Weeks, 3 Days

**Today is Forty Five Days,
which are Six Weeks
and Three Days,
of the Omer**

הַיוֹם חֲמִשָּׁה וְאַרְבָּעִים יוֹם שֶׁהֵם
שִׁשָּׁה שָׁבוּעוֹת וּשְׁלשָׁה יָמִים לָעֹמֶר

Day 46

6 Weeks, 4 Days

**Today is Forty Six Days,
which are Six Weeks
and Four Days,
of the Omer**

הַיוֹם שִׁשָּׁה וְאַרְבָּעִים יוֹם שֶׁהֵם
שִׁשָּׁה שָׁבוּעוֹת וְאַרְבָּעָה יָמִים לָעֹמֶר

Day 47

6 Weeks, 5 Days

**Today is Forty Seven Days,
which are Six Weeks
and Five Days,
of the Omer**

הַיּוֹם שִׁבְעָה וְאַרְבָּעִים יוֹם שֶׁהֵם
שִׁשָּׁה שָׁבוּעוֹת וַחֲמִשָּׁה יָמִים לָעֹמֶר

Day 48

6 Weeks, 6 Days

Today is Forty Eight Days,
which are Six Weeks
and Six Days,
of the Omer

הַיוֹם שְׁמוֹנָה וְאַרְבָּעִים יוֹם שֶׁהֵם
שִׁשָּׁה שָׁבוּעוֹת וְשִׁשָּׁה יָמִים לָעֹמֶר

Day 49

7 Weeks

Today is Forty Nine Days,
which are Seven Weeks,
of the Omer

הַיוֹם תִּשְׁעָה וְאַרְבָּעִים יוֹם שֶׁהֵם
שִׁבְעָה שָׁבוּעוֹת לָעֹמֶר

www.ingramcontent.com/pod-product-compliance
Lightning Source LLC
Chambersburg PA
CBHW041120120626
46547CB00019B/2781